# Mythological Poems

First Published: 2023
By TNC Press
First Edition
ISBN: 978-1-9993715-4-8

https://williamcooke.net

# Mythological Poems

William Cooke

TNC Press
2023

*'Whither is thy beloved gone, O thou fairest among women? whither is thy beloved turned aside?'*

## Not to Touch the Earth

Be willed! To touch the earth, or not?
The quick ascent—single concern.
Broken fortitude, fractured rock,
Alone, a precise path discerned.

To tumble to the earth in shock;
Giving up the ghost, exorcised
By broken rope at Eagle's Perch,
Brutal, earth-rendered, natural church.

Step by step, past the Muse's field.
Trespassing this route to the top,
Increasing my indulgent yields;
Ambrosial debts to the gods.

Then, slow into a world yet sealed
To mortal hands on seams of rock,
Where, at the conquered throne of Zeus,
Calloused flesh fixes its pursuit.

But then, to touch the Earth or not?
The question is, 'could I ascend
Beyond the snowy surface rock,
Bird-like?' My mortal form pretends.

Whereupon I touch this earth, not
For a moment more than... Distend!

Fly from here like mortal gases
And jump in Icarine madness.

## The Witch of Colchis

Twined by the bounds of all I know,
From the land to the marginal sea we plough,
In chase of a world that may be home
Set by stars on the meditative path;
To the Kartvelian Kingdom—
No longer Europe, Asia less—
And at that crossroads, East and West,
I've come again on the Argo's quest.
The troubled work of troubled sails
And troubled travels up mountain trails
They are the toil of renewed Jason
The one who seeks the Witch of Colchis.

Her form: of night. She speaks many things;
The Third of May, the archetypes.
Dark chthonic female other
Of unbound energy, mere men quiver.
In her stead, I find instead
A stranger to become a lover
Whose bow lips and heart face betray her
As a daughter of the Kartvelian Kingdom.
And at that crossroads West and East
I've come for the Golden Fleece.

I begged her, come with me—
Out of love, come.
Bring to me enchanted wines
And kisses of violent intensity.
But bound to the land and twined in vines,
To the sea, I saw her go.
Fixed in a loop she still called home
Set by stars on the meditative path;
From the Kartvelian Kingdom—
No longer Europe, Asia less–
I left with a useless, gold-stained pelt.

## Lament

*Non dulce sed decorum est in hiemi mori*

I was aware that time was not our friend,
Yet had no idea how many knives she held,
When she gave us each those memories
Of my small steps outgrowing you
In magnitude, until you were outpaced.

And I was impatient, to march the line,
I was a fool to toe that path until your death arrived.
There will always be the memories of autumnal skins of trees,
Burdening the trail we walked to school,
Rejuvenated in spring over again
To grow beyond us puny human things.

Then you were the last of your sort, for now.
The last old beloved whose life I must fear for.
For now.

Come round again,
I strip the silence from my speech and draw out
The tears that fill the moat, smothering my home,
In faded light, like liminal space.
Here I write and here I wait,
When I shouldn't have waited.
I ask you, turn the flood.
Please, come round again,

Open the gate.
The pictures are cold reminders
Of markers, just as much as rust.
They are no good!
When time can be cruel and kind
In equal lines of magnitude.
And how can life be granted
By unfair judges? Small and great sizes
Meted out by arbitrary justice?

Come, that I may say "goodbye"
And kiss your cheek.
Come round again with unblinded eyes
That see me clear and bright.
Come because I ask for more—

Never were three decades enough
Nor nine nor ninety more.

Time, for all her boundless glory,
Is a tightfisted whore with mortal lives.
Would you return if you could?
I ask too much of you,
When I did not dare return in time!

My interest is paid—
I'll see my moat filled,
I'll reap my harvest,
Ergotised and rough.
And more than this,
I shall slouch toward
The flames, which pick at you,
Unburdened by their warmth.

What time gives is a strange circle:
Demanding you retreat into the shell of eternity,
The same shell I was pulled from screeching
And will return yet, as formless void
One before your eyes and one mine…

The quiet grave is cold in January;
In it, only threaded roots cling to life.

## The Shipwreck of Saul of Tarsus

Maltese! Maltese! Monstrous seas
Where the wrath of the gods grows real.
From where the bent horizon recedes,
Comes the ship of Saul of Tarsus.

Shackled below in the Roman hold
Writhing and screaming, a storming crescendo,
An enemy most vile is scheming—
That zealous beast is Saul of Tarsus.

Maltese! Beware! Fear not the seas
But the earnest invasion from Galilee
And the *love* of the Nazarene
Soon unleashed by Saul of Tarsus.

The wretched creature pinned to wrecked cypress battens:
A tyrant loosed from the seaweed's pattern
Spewing his hatred for the rising sun.
Flee that shipwrecked beast from Tarsus.

## Untitled #1

In the thick of my own unborn chaos
I give birth to stars!
They will hail me henceforth,

Like they hailed Achilles, then
And in the far-off foreverlands, they quake
As I give the last of my music to you.

## The Tarantella Dancers

Look! The lowlands
Of the route
That birthed me,
Have given way
To rock wrought chapels
And well-baked roots.

And distant high-perched villages,
Like raptors over scrub,
Stand for stone-known centuries
Outside of human life.
Their hanging ways and walls
Of high-held houses;
Cobbled streets rubbed smooth
By human feet.

Look! A pilgrim on his holy route—
Gasping knight in open gate,
Where sun-drenched skins
Seek the shade's respite
And all the quiet of the day
Bounced by shorn-short gorse
The Echo's earth, and climbing ivy leaves.
Here frightening similarities,
Repetitions of home and overseas
Images I've always seen.
The ancient signs in foreign tongues
Shards of elder dreams
Whose designs, ideas precede
Those young women
I soon shall see.

Obscured by red and white dress cloth.
Framed hips, south of black doublets.
Proud stomps with hands on skirts
And chins aloft.
Their fine forms are far along
The cobbled hill, I'm rising up.
Slowly on, where drums unite
The driving, beating, girlish feet
Bare upon the baking road
And thrashing hands, on tambourines.

## The Fire Spirits

At the roof of the world,

Jinn amongst the bagged trash
Thrown aside on lust's demise
Twenty storeys to the brown river's thrash.

Her spirit of laughter here

Nests, her spirit of fire hurls
Discomfort for our interlocking legs—
Twenty storeys down to the water's curls.

The unbuilt block where sunrise dwells

Guarded from tumbling by the window's heft
Once. Once more. I do not come again.
Fate's arrows shot, there are no stories left.

## Thy Soul is as Gold Leaf

Thy Soul is as gold leaf hammered thinly
Burning as bright before burnishing as
Those moments fore twilight; sun crowned kingly.
My soul is as brass, tarnished it has.

Thou hast upon thee fragrance of Orchids
So earthy and human. Imperfectly
Perfect—thy scent, sends deft arrow Cupid's
To that folly of mine, that longs madly.

Thy worth is far greater than God's Kingdom
And thy name's syllables far sweeter still.
Thy love unobtainable does not come;
Thou hast cast my lot, rolling rocks uphill.

And from thy garden I'm ever cast out
Clued on to truth, on thy face was no doubt.

## Untitled #2

Go
Run,
Swim.
Set freedom as your north.

Ride the beast.
Slay the beast.
Be the beast.

## I am of the Sea

I am of the sea…
Heartache; the dimming figure ships in dying light—
The horizon fights
To keep all matter of the past in frame
And show the world's wanderers the way.
And I am of the sea, serene and still
Filled of siren song…

My lover is a broken sail
Cast upon the driftwood and the flotsam in the waves
That the merfolk's fleeting fingers
Pull into their murk enclaves.

And I am of the sea, serene and still
Filled of siren song.
Where the hidden currents drag the dead ones deep.
Aye! I am of the sea, made of breaking waves
That plunder worldly wonders.

I am all the cliches of the sea my lover loves, and more;
I am the seawall that keeps erosion from her human shores.

## Sabbath

Why has God given me so many Sundays?
An eternal injustice that I must rest
But also, I will die.

He has the time and temper
For everlasting rest
Not I.

## Maudlin

The disorder I spew and the weightless lines—
Rolling forth like cornstalks or summer vines.
They are the fruit I brew and boil to heavy drink
That clouds the sorrow of the fearful grip,
And jeering, bright buds above at Lisi Lake.

Where the wind blows out and the cold declines,
You and I are alike, in that my heart is leaden-tied to yours.
Now I am away and for all the day's hours—
Reflecting exile in polished, silvered masks
Is no straightforward mark or act, no stamped fact...

Nor is it what I needed, wanted, nor asked
As here on the rock the wines grow sour at last.

## Black Mountain

We went on down to Black Mountain
While death was upon us
A dark dog nipping at our heel.
We'd gone to seek our bounty;
But came upon the darkened passes,
Which opened out to Gaia
And sky-high, timeless churches.
How we poised ourselves for riches!
When Heaven, she opened fire,
And the firmament bellowed
Down hail and beat us,
And shed the tears of witches.

In our view now, the foothills
And the granite corpse of arches,
Which defined harmful Black Mountain.
"In you, we'll find our bounty."
Cried the prospector, Jeremiah.
But I knew truer that storms
Are ill auspices, born of water.
Yet Uranus did not crack the cloud
And ravens they did fly around
Like little monsters willing
That the welkin would ring death for us
And drown us in our path,
'Fore the august bulk of Black Mountain.

Death's brood upon the passes' walls
Death's drakes they did recall.
But each cold inch of stone,
Which stands so proud upon Black Mountain,
Drives each heart but onward.

Through any inch of stone that could be dug,
Jeremiah, dig he did.
The deepest pit there ever was.
But for the shaft's descent into her heart
Oh! We derived the path of death.
But toil laid our fears down.
That sweat—How it did beat my brow
As my pickaxe swung down
And Empyrean heaven gave her tears
In the baking heart of Black Mountain.

## The Slaver's Ship

In new light, they came and went
As ghosts in mist, when
Their hatchets swung
Eddies and vortices in the still air
Silent at first.

Erupting, then, through veils of smoke
Carried by a vicious lust
Their hatchets struck
On the latches and slats.
Still, she sat.
Serene as an effigy,
Her clothes torn up.

I watched my love carried off
For an unlived life on the Barbary Coast.
Look away, look away
Carried over the waves.
She goes off to a cruel place.
Grappling hands over her white breasts.
Cool as ice, their gaze
Her flesh.

I watched my love carried off
And daren't budge.
Hid across the field of cracked skulls
And flowing blood.
Look away, look away
Carried over the waves.
She goes off to a cruel place.
Do not look, despair instead.

## Love's Process

Lust came riding on a wind
Over the landfills,
On a whirlwind
Through the quivering fields,
To the Collines
In the night
Like Rome to the Sabines.

Came thundering, Love, like
Tied together shoestrings
Stumbling, shambling wreck.
The despoiling of all Nanking
Or Toward Yerevan
Like the Turk came
In the high heat.

Love led lump-throated
Into the courtroom
For overcoming me.
Love was hanged
After love was tried.

## My Anima

That you may be twenty-two hundred miles from me
Or prior engaged and guilt-ridden from coming to me
In the drunken stupor of each kiss and caress
(Where I am no better than thee)
Is of little concern in matters that feature such profundities.

You feel it, like me,
The outrageous pull of "meant to be"
And I am no prophet of fate,
No destiny-monger in shabby shawls.
I can be a vicious man,
Who burns whatever blocks him in.
I have clawed over a broken pit of limbs
To be just here, and then to have
This futile chase for some gone ghost
That was no picnic…

I traversed the world for you.
Gave up half a grave
A sentence of strangulation by the vine.
I sweated panicked in a plane for you.
And I didn't tell you
(Nor ever will unless you note this poem is for you.)
I emerged unwelcome in your head
But you came to me as the divine image of woman
The better side of potentiality, "tempus fugit—"
A Janus-face staring back at me.
Many idealised images have haunted my dreams
Poltergeisting themselves through my psyche
I have lived a life—
I am a fighter; and also, a fleer
You are neither— ever fixed in the same place
Since we came to be.

I wanted to drag you onto an island
From the bottom of your champagne sea
Wanted to kindle that potential.
I'd let you burn as I have also burned for you,
In the fevered dreams, I dream of thee.
But is this what you want or need? Is this my place?
I dare not press for more
Stopped by a young boy's fear,
That you may disappear as an icon pinned to a sacred wall.
But it is not for me to tense that thread of fate and make it wire.

Aren't you eternal?
Some kind of mirror of me?
Locked and bound in some reflected image born of youth
If you are what I want you to be.
The divine image of all women that outpours
And those that pour into me marked you
As a sacred thing.

Those high cheekbones and flat lips and the roman nose
A stern and solemn face, laughing only with correct gravity
(Is it weird that you are somewhat like me?)
And you are vulgar and drunk and revolutionary,
You are a case of what a warm night,
And an opera and a little drink can begin
With that quiet Kartvelian creak
That silences your wants and needs.
I whither. With or without you there is little life here
Away from the home I started to build.

And you too, tell me of sterile things that build no truth,
Bring nothing of the woman I am sure you must be.

## La Pietà

Mother, hold me like I dared not ask
In life. A crumbling form of chalk
In the unexplorèd wildness of the goddess death.
Her small and sickly impish brother
Lives in my stinking guts.

Asking how the line of salt was wetted
seems fruitless now;
An endeavour of the wretched thinking.
Your agony is great, mine over.

I—the formless, faithless denier—
Never sought the gift, nor ever could.
This wound consumes my side and seeps
A stagnant blood, and bile-marred breath
Spills forth.

They never ask, the children never ask.
Death, death, the destroyer does not consume.
She wants too much—
A cataclysm of time rages in my sleepless chest.

## Anaxagoras Looking on The Milky Way

"All this, one day, may reveal itself to me
When I erode in my constituent pieces.
I pray thee, life, hurry on!

They beg for me, these mysteries."

## The Fouling Ceremony

Long years ago, she woke
And she did not wake from sleep
But some sleeping sickness derived beneath;
Sleepwalking into a Gomorrah
That rained down sulphur on me
The temple seams unpeeled
And our home's hearth broke.

I never believed what was taught—
That God breathed life in me
And of my rib, she was born.
Certainly, it is she who precedes!
Doubtlessly, from her, the meaning pours
Endlessly, from her, it bleeds.

But, for *her*, I *was* cast out:
I had found paradise and left.
By the time I got to the city shrines,
The flat skyline, decayed, bereft
Like the houses of blessèd Palestine,
Reached the dead scrub's endless heft
And where prickly pears pierced the earth and climbed,
Something of me had breathed a final breath.

II

That was the land of Saint John's knights
And it was vile, wasted land on a wretched rock
Unlike what I had loved.
No water flowed and the people barked mad
Like waiting dogs for their commands.
There, the sacred son—so often imitated—
Was absentee, made only in dogmatic crosses
And the remnants of a glorious past
Lay hemmed in tents by order of the bosses
Just out of reach of the sea.

Just out of reach of the sea;
There some smell hangs long
On some balcony (our balcony,
Cut from the thin wall and railed with rust.)
Despite the red wind rising on the streets.

She was one of 'the ones'
But I fucked *it*, more than I fucked *her*

And that was the crux—
I dreamed of dreaming more than dreaming any dream.

The old tottering with the helpless in tow,
Bring about the desire that yawns from half of me.
To unify the broken, separated pieces of our being.

Yet, I am a squanderer. A serial squanderer.
I am a dead man in living man's muscles.
Hemmed in by order of the On-High
Sewn into stiff fasciæ
Whose bidding I do,
They bid me hold onto you
In the simoom, while the wet red dust piles up.

## III

Our love was long
But I grew ready to mourn you
And I mourned while you were a still effigy
Beside me.

I wrote your epitaph upon my maps and charts:

*"Therein, like death's designs and dreams*
*And Samson's toppled temple beams*
*The opposites, taut, on us lean.*
*Doubtlessly, from you, the meaning pours,*
*From me, the mourning streams."*

## Duende

Ochre mist on well-ridden roads
Over to adobe abodes, and bars of tiles
And orange alcoves, where we watch the women dance.

Spanish earth is Spanish life.
But soul is more than earth and life;
Raven hair and rippling pleats,
The stomping feet of Al-Andalus.

Overcome by sweat and drunk,
We watch the women dance with lust.

Clapping hands, rolling eyes,
Nostrils flaring by candlelight,
Chevaline and almost replete
Of air in stretching lungs;
Taut frames below taught tongues,
Which utter sacred words
When lost in love of living air.
Spirit; or soaring Geist
Under a restless moon in fevered night.
The red skirt riding on the hip
Exposing flesh well, yet poorly lit
By low lanterns, smoking wisps—

Overcome by sweat and drunk
We watch the women dance with lust.

## Untitled #3

Down from the perch, coils coming to rest
Creaking torque of self-similar scale
The dragon guards its high hoard
Circumscribed by claw and tail
The seeker seeks his pale reward
A dispersing jewel in the lizard's crest.

## Conception

With—
Pregnant force
At the noon, before

At the pivot's moment.
There lie beyond us:
Worlds of dry grass
On the wind dried bank.
And enter we,
To a terrorshow of
yellowing straw.
I hear beneath the ground creak
The itch on flesh,
A reddening welt.
The everfading wind
Over our dry course,
On the wind-dried bank.
The idle features,
Heaven's song dispersed
Each particulate act,
Every ancient measure:
Inside the fertile crescent
The opening walls,
Each potent motion
On the wind dried bank.
Do not damn us,
Condemn not us,
For we are wind dried wings
In guilty riot and intrepid act.
Entangled in rushes,
On the wind dried bank.

## Untitled #4

Iridescent Euphrates, spilling from you
Pishon of your spine!
God need not make from me some vulnerability
That is formed in you,
Already given breath by your charming flesh.

## Untitled #5

This gap, which belies wide eyes
Once faithful enough in love and lost
As a child in life, thrown
Beyond the dishonest ties
Upon the sacramental host.
The seed was sown.

The exercises that have grown
And sprouted dead lust below the breeze
In a world of your own claim.
Speak of the Grendaline frown,
Bearing through dim light through trees
Everything in the world is you
From far down.

The mine's grey karst
To the ringing birdsong.
I know you loved me
Until you didn't
And then I knew that too
But I dared not break my lips to question
What I feared to know at all.

### The Pain of Patience

I am waiting and waiting
I do nought but wait
For a time and a place
When the nightin-

Gales buster and shake
The new life to wake.
Here in this room
I wait for the heralds of Spring—
From your cold sleep awake!

## Alyssia

Blue light is what wakes me
When all others are long awake
And I stay in crouched wait.
They suck the air, my lips, they smack
Around my desire, the water that cures
And quenches the burning.

Life doles out no quarter nor favours.
Every man drowns in the same muddy water
As his persecutors.

I read these faded words in rune scripts
I saw the sadness when they addressed a different name
The Spirit lurked and lived through you but feared the world.
Nothing moved in me.
You asked the secrets of the haven.

October cried, nor did I answer the prayers of any solemn child
That knows that fear lurks in the ruined wilds.
Around to July, and things have changed
You are not exactly mine.

Your heart was my garden and I overworked it,
Grew tired and set it on the path to vine
In the passing time.
Out of mine, violence grows
And it is more beautiful than poppies
Or roses.
Thank the nourishing bones!
I lived as long as I did
But no more do I
Long to be.

A subject of divine order
Then a test upon the heart's weight.
I believed it necessary
Something to taunt this soul…
I believed it was senseless suffering
Then nothing.

I walk through this scene like a ghost.
they ask:
What is it you want?
I want the world to listen when my name is spoken.

Or any recognition I can muster.
I thought I discovered you
or wanted to. I wished I had.

Continuance;
Here a heart with no eyes lives
In with the magi,
Blood is wept and worms digress.
To live with her.
An apple rests.
But all these stories are futile.
Why inspire when I'd rather terrorise
Myself, with all the frescos of shame,
I'd long conjured up?

They prayed me: leave it there
In fate's clumsy hands,
Daft as a child's fat fists reaching in the cage
For a quaking canary,
And if they continue in this vein?

The thinking erodes—your face is weathered
By the road, my life veers far from you. Untethered
from my place, the detail fades.

Over your humanity, I chose sour persimmon.
The taste lingers, not long.
Are you my means or my end?
I am afraid of what goes on behind your doors.
When beyond mine, the boring dwell
With the bored in tow.
These fruits of ash create but stone.

## The Ship of Theseus: A Poem to Survival

Things grow and shed
Their overcoats and inner threads;
And piece by piece a ship becomes
Another thing more than its sum.
When Theseus he changes sails,
Arrives again, alters ropes.
A rotting plank is replaced
That his ship may stay afloat
And all that stored away for scrap
Awaits the day he comes back.
To build a boat…
But which is which or where is where?
Age old wisdom draws not near!

Heraclitus goes down to bathe,
Sees the water, rolling wild and fierce.
Sees a truth of the world as is, proclaims
'The river never is the same.'
And a ship rebuilt does it retain
Identity or become another thing?

When your father fucked you, I know it hurt
Mine fucked me too with hollow words.
Everyone begins again
Grows untouched skin.
Hair that hid you, nails to defend
All those renew in turn.
When you are no longer what you once were
Lost the old you to the earth
And nourished roots that stir,
Learned your lesson, given birth
Reached understanding through strife and work—
Is a ship, with pitch replaced, the same or different to before?
What of a plank, a faded sail?
Changed nuts and bolts, do they create?

You feel the same, but you have changed,
Untouched but to hands held dear,
Your identity is not so fixed
That you should hold onto any guilt
You, continually renewed,
Are not a product of a father's sin.
You are alive, each seven years reborn,
Again, again.

## A Burial

I dig my trenches with the wrong side to the sun
And cower, masking myself from the stellar might
Westward they face, guarding from the dying day
Whose allhours scatter over me broad light.
I was born back to front
From the cistern, I wander blind, hands out,
Eyes off, and feeling for the pillars that block my route
Hesitating at the arch, in its apex: light of foot
I pivot on the heel, aiming with the right eye closed to shoot
In the dream of the hunt.

Dead men, dead men, dead men
Bleached white by the shambling feet of eternity
Calcined by the hot summers, where baked bone recedes.
I lie by you in the unexplored meadow.
I am at ease with you...
Visions of the rust, I am encased
Head to toe by the worms of love
And the older vision (that is you!)

I learnt a thing or two—
About the bigger process of which I am an agent
Through which destruction flows, is channelled,
And grinds, and erodes me.
I sought my answers from the ecstatic rolling
That gripped and rolled me into my tightest form
Of unrolled steams that dissipate to the lolling,
Tuneless breeze of the Dionysian Ætheling
Gasping an unthinkable affront.

## Alexandria

In Alexandria, A lighthouse.
Seemed eternal to a boy,
A man,
To an empire

Until its fall.

## To Diana

I'd love to think I outdrew you,
Once pursued into the bramble of lust
Whither we grew stuck.

I loved you as I told you,
That was no liar's heist.
Nor a matter of trust.

And to think of you, sitting,
Weeping into your hands,
On my doorstep…

I've a sordid history of regrets,
As thick as forest,
Into which pursuit grew rough.

That was the one,
When your bow lips misspoke
And spouted love.

While I grew white and old
And all afraid to look
At your stern brow.

And let you go…
Into a world away from anything
Either had ever known.

And my vile arrows,
Slicked their poison in the wound.
But the corruption hardly crept.

## The Waiting Room

I have always felt that I am waiting for my life to begin.
Hindered by lines
Yellow lines, blurred lines
Lines in the sand and white lines
That intersect with the travesties I deny in being.

For I am waiting to begin again
In the waiting room
That calls this soul from the depths
To the waiting world.
The soul starts its journey
Light. Noise.
Bright light. Wild noise
Warped by the lights of some electric room
The waiting ends
And I begin;

Born and bald and bold
Screeching for the world
I was not always barred by lines
Not yellow lines, blurred lines
Lines in the sand nor white lines
And now I waste my precious time.

It makes me sick to drink and yet I drink.
It makes me dead.

Yet, I wait in the room that strings me in
With sacred secret cords that spill from syringe nibs
It makes me sick to be and yet I am.
And I shall always be...
A smudge on the page of eternity.
In league with all the tyrants,
Recurring war was always my name,
Struggle and strife
And lying.

Isn't it just some luck?
Right now, yellow lines and blurred lines
Lines in the sand and white lines
They bind and demarcate me,
While I wait to not be fucked.

## Regime Change at Easter

Astyages, King of the Medes,
Has broken bread for his last feast.
He'd die a poet, poor and sad
Without a throne, lost and mad.

That old king with his lost lands
Came again in turn
Riding on in the changing world,
That thundered, as I sauntered through the breeze
Without regard for love.

I can assure you it is no joke
That while you believe things progress
Some things surely peak
And however mutable and enthralled
Of Pandemonium we may be
We were perfect! Then nothing more
Will raise above the broken throne
You sat upon and surveyed the kingdom
That was our home.

We bore no intrigue in our sadness
I wanted you for you,
Stellar and sublime
Where heaven met the rolling waters.

I speak of the flux.
Let the birdsong inundate us,
The roof of this world beyond—
The river at Balkh;
My Roxana on the white bench

Barefoot and feet at play
In the fountain at change.

## Sailing From Byzantium

The holy city, from my rowboat,
To the rear of me, consumed by fires.
The sacred slaughtered, the living
Left for the slaver's market.

The immutable golden artifice on broken branches
Sacked and left for blood-wet hands,
Singing not what was to come
But honey songs and sweetbriar
Thorns; among those bright roses,
Told the tale of the faded empire's fall.

And that lost country, jewels;
Marbles stripped away, traded
For somniferous wines, dulcet whore's quarters
Sensuous pleasures for threadbare cloaks of purple.
Was I sent as saviour here?

Because I also flee the yoke and scourge of The Ottoman Empire.

The last caught by the golden horn
And fang-like scimitars
Tines of dilemma's fork—
Death by drowning, slavery—
Rapine of the golden city,
Left an ember sea,
Which I had hoped to save.

But I find myself in fearful flight
Toward an exile's chains and shame.
So, I am sailing from Byzantium
Heart-sick to look back at thee
From the flotsam-filled and burning sea.

Rafts of nude, huddled forms afloat
Children in the water, drowning rats
Grappling at frayed ropes;
Frail, thin arms taken by the black.

These turning engines of eternity
Undo what a millennium of priests and sages sang
Then a day shall be, none longer know
What has passed, is passing, or to come.

## A Thank You

Dear Reader,

I want to thank you kindly for taking the time to get ahold of this work and read it. It would be disingenuous to wish that you enjoyed reading it as much as I did writing it, because the writing process is difficult and sometimes torturous. I hope it was a much more profitable experience for you! I value the time you have taken to engage with this short slice of mostly universal human experience that has chosen to emerge through me.

If you think this book would speak to any others, or if you wish to further explore its ideas, I ask that you take the time to share it. I ask that you take the time to engage in discussions, be it with your friends at home or over that miraculous communication tool, so embedded into our modern lives. Furthermore, if you wish to delve deeper into the ideas with me, I am more than open to it. I receive all messages with joy. I hope I will have the opportunity to hear the thoughts of some of you soon!

*William*

## About The Author

Hailing from England, *William Cooke* is a Poet, Essayist, and Storyteller. He retains a profound interest in Modern and Classical tales, including Mythology. His highest purpose is to raise the profile of Mythological thought in our spiritually hungry world via recounting the secrets from his many adventures and misadventures.

Influenced by Jungian Psychology and Existential Philosophy, his main aims are to explore the eternal human experience and bring it into order. This project is a life's work and is channelled through his writings.

www.ingramcontent.com/pod-product-compliance
Lightning Source LLC
LaVergne TN
LVHW050339160826
845677LV00014B/3695

* 9 7 8 1 9 9 9 3 7 1 5 4 8 *